Babies Come From... Where?!?

Funny Happens When Kids Explain Pregnancy & Birth

Kristi Porter

ISBN: 0692439056
ISBN-13: 978-0692439050

CONTENTS

Dedication

This book is dedicated to every parent, grandparent, and caregiver that entrusted me with the care and education of their child over the years.

We've all earned a good laugh.

And to the Happi Kamper Kids, the preschoolers at Community United Methodist Preschool, and the Power Play Kids, who all had a part in providing me with material for this book.

Keep smiling and providing those laughs!

The Story Behind This Book

Babies Come From… Where?!? is the result of hundreds of interviews with young children ages three to twelve, who were simply asked "Where do you think babies come from?" and allowed to answer freely, giving as much or as little explanation as they saw fit.

It began as part of a larger class project by teacher Kristi Porter and the children of Happi Kamper Child Care, located in North Muskegon, Michigan. Each child was to create an individual gift book for his or her parents, and *Babies Come From… Where?!?* was simply to be one chapter in each child's book.

Now, the individual answers of the Happi Kamper Kids, as well as those of the children at Community United Methodist Preschool, and the kids of Power Play Childcare have been combined. Their diverse, candid, and uncensored answers may surprise you, or even make you laugh out loud, as you get a quick glimpse into the amazing and intricate minds of some of the most delightful and fascinating children around. Enjoy!

PART I

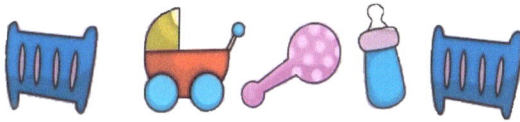

... Little tiny babies are in the mom's tummy. They wait and wait and grow and grow and make the mommy very fat. Then the mommy goes to the hospital and the doctor pushes really hard on her tummy and the baby goes flying right out! When the nurse catches it everyone is very happy. ~Emily, age 4.

~ * ~ * ~ * ~ * ~ * ~ * ~

... God puts a baby in the mom's tummy – unless he's busy, then Jesus does it. ~Olivia R., age 5.

~ * ~ * ~ * ~ * ~ * ~ * ~

... When moms get too fat a baby gets in there and eats the extra food. Then when they want to get out the doctor cuts up the moms stomach, grabs the baby and gives the mom stitches. Then the baby starts to walk and talk and yell and cry. A lot. ~Donovan, age 8.

~ * ~ * ~ * ~ * ~ * ~ * ~

... Babies crawl right out of a momma's belly. They don't like it very much in there, and when they finally get out they whine and whine about it! ~Fallon, age 3.

~ * ~ * ~ * ~ * ~ * ~ * ~

... Moms and Dads find a baby in the crib in the morning. They pick it up and look at it, and if they like it they play with it and keep it forever. If they don't like it they still have to keep it, but they put it back in the crib. ~Kali, age 4.

~ * ~ * ~ * ~ * ~ * ~ * ~

... The doctors push babies into a mom's tummy and make it stay for a while, then they push it back out. The babies don't like being pushed so you have to give it a bottle when it's born so it will shut up. ~Justine, age 5.

~ * ~ * ~ * ~ * ~ * ~ * ~

... Babies come from the blue store. Wait, that's for toy babies. Real babies come from Kindergarten, I think. You just have to go there and feed them and bring them home to Chelsea's room, NOT to my room, because I don't want to smell them. ~Shayna, age 3.

~ * ~ * ~ * ~ * ~ * ~ * ~

... Babies are made out of eggs and worms. First the mom has some eggs and then she gets some worms from the dad. Then when the worms get in the moms stomach they find the eggs and somehow they mix together and turn into a baby. I'm glad I'm not a girl, 'cause no way I'm ever gonna eat worms! ~Wesley, age 9.

... Jesus makes babies inside the mom's belly. Then the mom and dad get married so they have to leave the baby at the doctor's office for a couple of days. When they get done being married they go get the baby and take it home. ~Brielle, age 5.

~ * ~ * ~ * ~ * ~ * ~ * ~

... Babies grow in a mommy's belly. They grow bigger and bigger until the mom sings 'Pop Goes the Weasel' and then it just pops right out of there! ~Derek, age 4.

~ * ~ * ~ * ~ * ~ * ~ * ~

... Babysitters have all the babies. You just go and pick whichever one you want and bring it home and put it in the crib. Then it's yours. ~Cami, age 5.

~ * ~ * ~ * ~ * ~ * ~ * ~

... A doctor puts the baby in the mom's belly. Then her belly gets bigger and bigger and bigger until it breaks, and then it's your birthday! ~Denny, age 4.

~ * ~ * ~ * ~ * ~ * ~ * ~

... Babies come from a mom's tummy. They grow until her belly cracks open like an egg and the baby crawls out. ~Riley, age 4.

~ * ~ * ~ * ~ * ~ * ~ * ~

... My mommy gots a baby in her tummy. She said the doctor will take it out at Christmas, but I think maybe Santa Claus will help him. Then I get to see my new baby. His name is gonna be brother. ~Jake D., age 3.

~ * ~ * ~ * ~ * ~ * ~ * ~

... Babies are magical, kinda like leprechauns. You just find them in the house one day – they like sneak in there somehow. Then you have to keep it in the crib 'til 3:30. But then it's okay to take it downstairs and play with it.
~Josie H., age 4.

~ * ~ * ~ * ~ * ~ * ~ * ~

... First you have to sing 100 songs under the baby tree and then a baby will get in the mom's belly. Then the mom sings 100 more songs and the doctor will take it out of her belly. Then you have to change its diaper for 100 days and then the baby grows up. ~ Olivia, age 5.

~ * ~ * ~ * ~ * ~ * ~ * ~

... I don't really know how they get in there, but I do know they come out of a mom's tummy. I think the mom pushes on it when she gets tired of it kicking her, and then it just comes out somehow. The doctor has to look at it first, but if it looks good, then you can take the baby home.
~Ansley, age 4.

~ * ~ * ~ * ~ * ~ * ~ * ~

... Babies come from eggs. Eggs come from birds – or maybe a factory, I'm not sure. But the baby cracks the egg to get out and wears a parachute to fly down to its mom. Then she has to keep it. ~Ryan, age 4.

When a mom wants a baby she goes to a special nurse lady and she takes one out of the mom's tummy. But you have to leave the baby there for a day before you can bring it home. ~Gillian, age 4.

~ * ~ * ~ * ~ * ~ * ~ * ~

… The servants cut the mom's belly in half and pull a baby right out. Then later the mom takes it home.
~Trevor, age 4.

~ * ~ * ~ * ~ * ~ * ~ * ~

… You get a baby from the hospital. You have to buy them for $28. And if you buy a girl baby you get a toy. If you buy a boy baby you get a balloon. ~Hayden, age 4.

~ * ~ * ~ * ~ * ~ * ~ * ~

… Moms and dads drive far, far away to the rainbow place. Then they just walk in the door of the baby house and pick one baby to keep forever. They have to pay like $50 bucks for it, but then they can take it home. ~Lindy, age 4.

~ * ~ * ~ * ~ * ~ * ~ * ~

… Babies come from a momma's heart. I think they get out by pushing when the door is open, or maybe they try and reach out, I don't really know about that. But when they get out you have to wash them and play with them and take them places, like to the airport. ~Chase S., age 4.

~ * ~ * ~ * ~ * ~ * ~ * ~

… God sends a baby angel into the mom's tummy, and then it grows into a regular baby and just falls right out when it's ready. Then you have to hug it and take it home.
~Brennan, age 3.

~ * ~ * ~ * ~ * ~ * ~ * ~

... When a mom wants a baby she has to get a special birthday cake. The dad blows on the candles, and then the baby comes out of the cake and the mom and dad get to keep him forever. ~Austin L., age 3.

~ * ~ * ~ * ~ * ~ * ~ * ~

... God makes the baby inside the mom's tummy, but it gets bored in there so the mom goes to the hospital for two weeks until it comes out. ~Mickayla, age 4.

~ * ~ * ~ * ~ * ~ * ~ * ~

... First a mom marries someone, then she gets pregnant, and then she has a baby. And only ladies can have babies! ~Dominique, age 9.

~ * ~ * ~ * ~ * ~ * ~ * ~

... Babies crawl inside bellies when nobody is looking, I think. Then they crawl out and cry when they want to go home. Then the mom has to go to the mall and buy some toys. ~Kayleigh A, age 3.

~ * ~ * ~ * ~ * ~ * ~ * ~

… Babies come from doctors. He gets 'em from his house and checks them out. If they cry he gives them to a mom to hold and take care of, if they don't cry he has to keep them for longer. ~Zachary S., age 3.

~ * ~ * ~ * ~ * ~ * ~ * ~

…You get babies from a special little room at the hospital. I think they just stay there until somebody buys them. I don't know how much a baby is gonna cost, because we're gonna have a baby and my mom and dad said they cost a lot, but we don't have it yet so maybe they are saving up for it. ~David, age 4.

~ * ~ * ~ * ~ * ~ * ~ * ~

… Babies crawl, crawl, crawl. They crawl right in the mommy's tummy and then they crawl right out. But if you give it toys it will probably stay out of there. ~Wes, age 4.

~ * ~ * ~ * ~ * ~ * ~ * ~

… You get a baby from the doctor. He takes it to the mom & dad's home in his doctor's car. Then the mom takes him to bed and the daddy puts the baby in the highchair and goes to watch TV. ~Garrett, age 4.

~ * ~ * ~ * ~ * ~ * ~ * ~

… God puts babies in all the mom's tummies. When they want to get out, the doctor at the hospital gives the mom a shot and then the baby can come out. Then you have to rock it, put it in bed, and make it go to sleep. ~Connor, age 4.

~ * ~ * ~ * ~ * ~ * ~ * ~

… Babies come from the grocery store. They cost five dollars for a girl baby and two dollars for a boy baby. You just buy 'em and bring 'em home and feed them pickles. ~Hailey, age 4.

~ * ~ * ~ * ~ * ~ * ~ * ~

… Mommies' tummies are full of babies. They just grow in there all the time. If she wants one to play with then the mommy goes to the doctor's office and he pulls one out so the momma can take it home and hold it. ~Claire, age 4.

~ * ~ * ~ * ~ * ~ * ~ * ~

… All I know is that the hospital people take it out of the momma's tummy and then you have to take care of it. ~Julia, age 4.

~ * ~ * ~ * ~ * ~ * ~ * ~

… Doctors put babies in a mom's tummy. I think he just unzips it and puts it in there. Then anytime you want to, you just unzip it again and take it back out. ~Clare, age 3.

~ * ~ * ~ * ~ * ~ * ~ * ~

…Babies come from a mom's stomach, and I *do* know how babies are made, but I don't want to tell you. Let's just say… the dad *gives it* to the mom. (the child then leaned forward and winked, before continuing) Then, when it's time to be born they go to the hospital and the baby shoots right out of the mom's *you know what*, and the doctor catches it. And that's all I've got to say about that! ~Korbin, age 9.

~ * ~ * ~ * ~ * ~ * ~ * ~

… Babies grow from seeds. You just plant them in the flowerpot and wait for them to grow up. Then you can just let them go play outside. ~Gus, age 4.

~ * ~ * ~ * ~ * ~ * ~ * ~

PART II

… Babies grow inside a mom's tummy. And did you know that the baby has a rope inside the tummy to hang onto so it don't fall out the mom's butt? ~William, age 5.

~ * ~ * ~ * ~ * ~ * ~ * ~

… Well, when the mommy and daddy get married the baby gets in the mom's tummy, 'cause that's the rule of married. After a while they go to the hospital and get the baby out. Then they have to take it home and rock-a-by it to sleep. ~Katie M., age 5.

~ * ~ * ~ * ~ * ~ * ~ * ~

… Babies come from Jesus. He makes them and gives 'em to the momma. She holds them, and plays with them, and changes their diaper. But daddies don't, 'cause they don't like stinky things. ~Chase E., age 3.

~ * ~ * ~ * ~ * ~ * ~ * ~

…A baby gets inside a moms stomach when she eats lots of good food and drinks lots of milk. After a while it grows big and it hurts the mom and kicks her so the doctor takes the baby out at the hospital. Then they let the baby rest in a

little bed. After a few weeks you take the baby home.
~Josh, age 7.

~ * ~ * ~ * ~ * ~ * ~ * ~

... The mom goes to the doctor and he shows her lots of babies. The mom picks a good one, like my sister Jenna, and brings it home. Then you have to give it medicine 'cause she might have an earache. When the baby is better she can play with boats. ~Brenden H., age 4.

~ * ~ * ~ * ~ * ~ * ~ * ~

... Fairies put babies in a mom's belly. Then the doctor cuts the belly a little bit and takes the baby out. You have to feed them baby food and milk and then leave them in their crib for a long, long time. ~Collyn, age 4 ¾.

~ * ~ * ~ * ~ * ~ * ~ * ~

... I don't really know how, but somehow a baby gets inside the moms belly and makes her fat. When she gets tired of being fat she just takes it out and gives it milk and makes it sleep in a carriage. ~Josie E., age 4.

~ * ~ * ~ * ~ * ~ * ~ * ~

... Moms go to the store and get a baby. Dads go fishing.
~Michael, age 5.

… Babies come from a mommy's tummy. When a mommy and daddy get married the baby gets in there. When it's time for the baby to come out, the mom lies on a table and the baby comes out from between the momma's legs. Then it goes to that one little room where all the babies are. Then if everyone is good they get to go home.
~Chelsea, age 8.

~ * ~ * ~ * ~ * ~ * ~ * ~

… Some weird people make the baby and put it in the mom's tummy when she's sleeping. Then the doctor takes it out when it's big and cleans it so the mom can put a diaper on it and send it to bed. ~Kayla U., age 4.

~ * ~ * ~ * ~ * ~ * ~ * ~

… Babies come from hospitals. The mom orders one and then just picks 'em up when they are ready. ~Sydney, age 4.

~ * ~ * ~ * ~ * ~ * ~ * ~

… God gives the babies to the doctor and he puts them in the mom's tummy. After a few weeks the baby is ready so the doctor reaches in the mom's tummy with his hand and pulls it right out. Then you have to put it in the crib and give it a blanket so it will go to sleep. ~Brett U., age 4.

~ * ~ * ~ * ~ * ~ * ~ * ~

…Babies grow in a mom's tummy. Then they kick and kick until they kick right out of there. Then you have to take care of it forever. ~Ethan, age 5.

~ * ~ * ~ * ~ * ~ * ~ * ~

… You go to the toy store and buy them. They cost $24 for a boy baby and $3 for a girl baby. Then you bring them home and put a diaper on them. ~Elizabeth, age 3.

~ * ~ * ~ * ~ * ~ * ~ * ~

… Babies come out of bellies. They get in there by pregnant, whatever that is. When the mom wants it to come out, she goes to the doctor and he cuts her belly open and takes it out. Then you have to take the baby home and take care of it 'til it's bigger like me. ~Brenden M., age 4.

~ * ~ * ~ * ~ * ~ * ~ * ~

… Babies come from big baskets. They just jump in there and the mom finds them when she comes home. Then she keeps them forever. ~Zack, age 3.

~ * ~ * ~ * ~ * ~ * ~ * ~

… Mommies have to eat a lot of eggs, and then the baby will grow in their belly. When the eggs run out the doctor cuts up the mom and takes the baby out of her belly. Then you have to go to the store and buy it toys. ~Chad, age 4.

~ * ~ * ~ * ~ * ~ * ~ * ~

… Babies come from bellies. They just surprise you in there! I know the mom goes to the hospital and the doctor gets the baby out of there, but I don't really know how they do all that. Then the mom can hold the baby and take them to lots of places, like Traverse City. ~Leah, age 5.

~ * ~ * ~ * ~ * ~ * ~ * ~

… A lady has to put a special thing on her belly so the baby gets in there. Then she puts a different thing on her belly and it gets right out of there. Then you have to put some super glue on her belly and rock the baby to sleep. ~Grace, age 3.

~ * ~ * ~ * ~ * ~ * ~ * ~

… Babies get into a mom's head and go down, down, down. They eat a lot and make the mom fat so the doctor takes it out and the mom takes it home. ~Luci, age 4.

~ * ~ * ~ * ~ * ~ * ~ * ~

… The doctor pushes on momma's belly and it makes a baby there. Then he pushes on it some more and it comes out. But it will be bloody! The doctor fixes momma's belly with some tape and daddy washes all the blood off. Then the momma can go home. And the baby too. ~Kelcie, age 3.

~ * ~ * ~ * ~ * ~ * ~ * ~

… Doctors use special tools to make babies. Then they give one to the mom when she goes to the hospital. ~Zachary M., age 4.

~ * ~ * ~ * ~ * ~ * ~ * ~

… Babies are in oceans. They swim in the water and moms and dads feed them and pet them and play with them. Then they pick one and take it home. ~Lily, age 4.

~ * ~ * ~ * ~ * ~ * ~ * ~

... I don't know how, but somehow babies get inside a mommies tummy. Then they go to the hospital and the doctor pokes the mommies tummy until he pokes it right out. Then you take it home. ~Cole, age 4.

~ * ~ * ~ * ~ * ~ * ~ * ~

... Babies come down with the snowflakes. The mom brings them in the house and takes care of them. When they get to be kids they tell the mom to just leave them alone and let them play. ~Christian, age 4.

~ * ~ * ~ * ~ * ~ * ~ * ~

... God puts babies in girl tummies. The doctors push the baby out when it's time to come out and then they wash it 'cause it has blood all over it. Then you have to put a hat on it and take it home. ~Isabelle, age 5.

~ * ~ * ~ * ~ * ~ * ~ * ~

... A mom buys the baby from the store and puts it in her tummy. Then the dad calls the doctor and he puts a little hole in the mom so the baby can get out. The baby is very happy to get out 'cause it did not like to see all the blood inside there. ~Noa, age 5.

~ * ~ * ~ * ~ * ~ * ~ * ~

… Other people put babies in the mom's tummy. Then she pushes on her tummy and the baby comes right out. You have to hold the baby and read it baby books and then put it in a cradle so he will go to sleep. But if it thunders outside he will wake up and cry. ~Haley, age 4.

~ * ~ * ~ * ~ * ~ * ~ * ~

… God disappears them into the mother's tummy. Then the doctor gets some scissors and gets the baby right out. You can hold them for a minute and then they take them to get fixed. When you bring the baby home you have to keep it forever. ~Kaleb, age 5.

~ * ~ * ~ * ~ * ~ * ~ * ~

… The doctor puts on gloves and pulls the baby out of the mom's pee-pee. Lots of blood comes out, too. Then you rock the baby and sing tree top to it and put on some music so it can go to sleep. Oh, and you have to feed it macaroni & cheese when it gets hungry. ~Natalie I., age 5.

~ * ~ * ~ * ~ * ~ * ~ * ~

… Babies come from someone else, I'm not sure who. Mom's have to go pick them up when they are ready and take them home. And you have to keep them inside.
~Cameron, age 4.

~ * ~ * ~ * ~ * ~ * ~ * ~

… Everybody has babies in their tummy. The babies stay inside your tummy until you are big enough to take care of it. Then they come out and you give them a bottle so they won't cry. ~Allie, age 5.

~ * ~ * ~ * ~ * ~ * ~ * ~

… Lots of babies grow in the mom's tummy. Then when the appointment meeting is, the doctors cut the belly and pull out three babies and put them on the floor and just roll them over to the nurse. The babies are really ugly when you look at them, but everyone says "oh what cute, cute, cutie babies." You have to go visit them every day, and after a few months you put them in a car seat and take them home and play with them and stuff. But you have to keep them forever until they grow up and die. ~Hunter, age 4. (brother to triplets)

~ * ~ * ~ * ~ * ~ * ~ * ~

… Babysitters bring a new baby to the hospital and put it in the mom's tummy. Then the hospital people take it out and give it to the mom when she wakes up. ~Jennie, age 4.

~ * ~ * ~ * ~ * ~ * ~ * ~

… Babies live in a old Grandma's house. Mommy goes there and gets one. That's all there is about that.
~Tommy, age 3.

~ * ~ * ~ * ~ * ~ * ~ * ~

… The moms and dads go to the hospital and do stuff and then they go home, but they have 'ta leave the baby at the hospital until Friday, then they get to take her home forever.
~Joey, age3.

~ * ~ * ~ * ~ * ~ * ~ * ~

… Babies come out of bellies. They grow from inside the momma for pretty much a year and then the mom goes to the doctor and gets checked out to get surgery. Then when that's done the mom carries the baby around to lots of places.
~Devin, age 8.

~ * ~ * ~ * ~ * ~ * ~ * ~

… The mom finds a tiny little baby under the leaves in the woods and the dad puts it in the mommy's tummy. When it grows bigger the doctor puts a little hole in the mom so the baby can get out, and then the doctor puts a Band-Aid on the mom. The baby is very happy to not see all the blood and guts inside the mom anymore and grows up to be a big girl.
~Holly, age 4.

~ * ~ * ~ * ~ * ~ * ~ * ~

… You go to the Walgreens store and way in the back they have a special shelf with all the babies on it. They cost about 90 bucks I think. You just pay and then take one home. Oh, and you have to buy diapers and bottles too.
~Meggan, age 5.

PART III

... Babies come out of a mom's tummy. They just get in there all by themselves, I don't really know how. But when the babies foot is sticking out, the mom knows to go to the hospital, and then the doctor will take them all the way out. ~Clark, age 4.

~ * ~ * ~ * ~ * ~ * ~ * ~

... Hmmm, I've never been asked that question before. Let me think... I know the mom has 'em in her stomach, and then they get out from the private parts. And that's all I have to say! ~Eric, age 6.

~ * ~ * ~ * ~ * ~ * ~ * ~

... You have to go to the doctor's house and ask him if you can buy one. A new baby costs $5.00 so you have to save up for a while. Then you bring them home and change some diapers and go to bed with them. I don't know how much a old baby costs. ~Kayleigh W., age 4.

~ * ~ * ~ * ~ * ~ * ~ * ~

... Babies grow in a mom's tummy when she drinks lots of water. Then the mom unbuttons her belly button and takes it out. Then she just buttons her belly button again until the next time. ~Natalie L., age 4.

~ * ~ * ~ * ~ * ~ * ~ *

... Jesus is in charge of puttin' babies in the mom's tummies. But the doctor is in charge of gettin' 'em out. Dads just get to carry the baby home. ~Troy, age 5.

~ * ~ * ~ * ~ * ~ * ~ * ~

… Babies come out of a mom's tummy. The babies have lots of fun in there but when they get bored then the doctor puts the mom's feet on some magnet things and it sucks the baby right out. Then it's not so much fun, 'cause you have to change its diaper and all that stuff. ~Caleb R., age 4.

~ * ~ * ~ * ~ * ~ * ~ * ~

… The dad puts sperm in the mom and it fertilizes the mom's egg. Then it turns into a baby. The baby comes out when they're born between the mothers legs. Then they cut off the umbilical cord and then they spank the baby so it will breathe. Everybody stays in the hospital for a week and then goes home. ~Andy, age 11.

~ * ~ * ~ * ~ * ~ * ~ * ~

… Babies live in a big nest. When they get hungry, they just fly right out of there and go to the mom and dad's house. They feed it potatoes and milk and put it in a crib and keep it forever. ~Renee, age 3.

… Doctors grow babies in a special room at the hospital. When a mom wants a new baby she goes and picks out a good one and they get borned. But she still has to keep the old baby, too! ~Thomas, age 4.

~ * ~ * ~ * ~ * ~ * ~ * ~

… Teeny tiny invisible babies climb right into the mom's belly button and make her belly get fat. Then the doctor has to open up the belly button to make the baby come out. He keeps the baby for a while and cleans it off, and then the mom takes it home. ~Kayla M., age 3.

~ * ~ * ~ * ~ * ~ * ~ * ~

… I think moms just keep a baby in their belly all the time. Then one day she goes to the doctor and he takes it out. But he has to take a picture of it first to make sure it's ready. Then you can take it home. ~Drake, age 4.

~ * ~ * ~ * ~ * ~ * ~ * ~

… Babies come from special baby stores. They are all at the store and moms and dads pick one they like and pay for it. It costs $20 for a girl and $7 for a boy. Then they can take it home, but they have to feed it bananas and bottles every day. ~Lauren, age 4.

~ * ~ * ~ * ~ * ~ * ~ * ~

… When it rains outside they just fall right down from the clouds! Then you can bring them in the house and give them a towel and keep them. ~Anthony H., age3.

~ * ~ * ~ * ~ * ~ * ~ * ~

… Babies get in a moms tummy when God puts it there. It gets out when the doctor cuts the mom's tummy open and takes the baby out. Then the doctor tapes moms' tummy shut with some super strong special tape. When it's all sewed up you can take the big huge Band-Aid off and go home.
~Charles, age 6.

~ * ~ * ~ * ~ * ~ * ~ * ~

…Babies come from stomachs. The mom eats them and then she throws up a lot so the dad takes her to the hospital to get them out. ~Elli, age 4.

~ * ~ * ~ * ~ * ~ * ~ * ~

… Well, babies can come from lots of places… like hospitals, heaven, and tummies. The mom eats some special food and it grows into a baby. Then the hospital people talk to heaven and God lets the baby come out.
~William G., age 5.

~ * ~ * ~ * ~ * ~ * ~ * ~

… Babies come from cribs. The mom puts them in there on Saturday. On Sunday she gives it a ladder so it can climb right out of there. Then you have to give it baby toys, like dinosaurs and stuff. ~Brett H., age 3.

... When a daddy and a momma get married, they both get a baby in their tummies. The daddy keeps his in his tummy forever, but the momma goes to the doctor and he pokes her and pokes her 'til the baby comes out. Then you put a blanket over its head and go home. ~Caleb M., age 4.

~ * ~ * ~ * ~ * ~ * ~ * ~

... Babies come from milk. You mix some with special water and drink it and then it grows into a baby in your tummy. The doctor gets it out when it's big enough and gives it some corn. They you have to put it night-night.
~Katie C., age 4.

~ * ~ * ~ * ~ * ~ * ~ * ~

... Walmart! They cost about $50. I want 100 when I grow up. But I'm gonna need lots of diapers! ~Delaney, age 3.

~ * ~ * ~ * ~ * ~ * ~ * ~

... Babies are inside eggs. The baby eats all the food in the eggs and then pops out of the egg and goes in the tummy. Then it pops out of the tummy and is really tiny and the mom takes it home and puts it in bed. In the morning you have to get it out of the crib 'cause it will be screaming.
~Emilia, age 4.

~ * ~ * ~ * ~ * ~ * ~ * ~

... Doctors make the babies, and then the babies just lay around in the mom's belly until the doctor gets a big knife and gets it out. You have to keep it, so you buckle it in a car seat and drive home. ~Landon, age 5.

~ * ~ * ~ * ~ * ~ * ~ * ~

... The Easter Bunny brings them. You don't even have to leave a basket or nothing! He just hops, hops, hops from way far back from my house and brings a new baby and puts it in the crib. And he still gives me candy too! ~Jennifer, age 3.

~ * ~ * ~ * ~ * ~ * ~ *~

… Babies come from heaven. The seeds in a mom's tummy get mixed up together by God and that makes a baby. Then the mom goes to the doctor and he does the tummy thing and gets the baby out. The nurse wraps it up in a blankie so it won't be freezing and then the mom can bring the baby home and love it forever. ~Rhiannon, age 4.

~ * ~ * ~ * ~ * ~ * ~ *~

… Babies float down from the air and get in the mom's tummy when she's not looking. I don't know how they get out, maybe they just float out when the mom is sleeping, but when they do you have to spank them and put them to bed. ~Makayla, age 4.

~ * ~ * ~ * ~ * ~ * ~ *~

… Big fat people have babies in their tummy. They just crawl right in there and stretch and stretch so they will fit. When they crawl out again the mommy is happy and they live happily ever after. ~Noah, age 3

~ * ~ * ~ * ~ * ~ * ~ *~

… It's Magic. First moms eat lots of good stuff and it magically turns into a baby in her tummy. Then the doctor cuts a circle in the mom and takes off her skin so the baby can come out. Then the doctor puts some magic medicine on the mommy so her skin will grow back. The hospital guys make the mom take the baby home and keep it until it turns into a grown-up. ~Jimmy, age 4.

~ * ~ * ~ * ~ * ~ * ~ * ~

… Babies grow in tummies. The doctor cuts the tummy with a big, big knife and takes the baby out. They give it shots and then the baby can go home with its mommy.
~Jezica, age 4.

~ * ~ * ~ * ~ * ~ * ~ * ~

… Babysitters make all the babies. You can pick a sister or a brother, but you have to be nice to them until they are three. Then they go to school and get new big bird sheets on their bed until they are grown up. Then they move out.
~Emma, age 3.

~ * ~ * ~ * ~ * ~ * ~ * ~

… God makes the babies and puts them in tummies. Just mom tummies, though. Then the doctor opens the tummy and takes the baby out and wipes the blood off so you can take it home and put clothes on it - 'cause nobody wants a naked baby running around! ~Dallas, age 4.

~ * ~ * ~ * ~ * ~ * ~ * ~

… Babies just start in a mom's tummy. Then when they are one year old they get born and have to get out of there. That's all I know. ~Erin, age 4.

~ * ~ * ~ * ~ * ~ * ~ * ~

… My grandma says that you find babies hiding underneath giant leaves on a cabbage plant in the garden, but

I know that's not true - 'cause we learned about it at school. I think my grandma is getting a little silly in the brain, don't you? ~Marilynn, age 12.

~ * ~ * ~ * ~ * ~ * ~ * ~

… I think babies come from the hospital. When you want one you just call up the hospital lady and she puts a blanket over the one you want and puts a diaper on them. Then she saves them so people like us can go and pick them up. ~Anna, age 4.

~ * ~ * ~ * ~ * ~ * ~ * ~

… God puts a baby in the mom's tummy with magic. But the people at the hospital want it out of there so they push on it 'til it comes out. Then you give it a bottle and take it to the store and buy some crayons. ~Cassidy, age 4.

~ * ~ * ~ * ~ * ~ * ~ * ~

… The doctor puts a baby in the mom's belly with some special medicine. Then he pushes real hard and gets the baby back out and gives it a pacifier. ~Jake, age 4.

~ * ~ * ~ * ~ * ~ * ~ * ~

… I know this one. Babies come from tummies. They just grow in there until it's big, then they get so big that they grow right out of there! Then you lift the baby up and take it to

your house. You have to tuck it into bed so it will go to sleep and when it wakes up you have to give it a flower.
~Alec, age 4.

~ * ~ * ~ * ~ * ~ * ~ * ~

Somebody, I think maybe like God, sends the baby into the mom's tummy. Then one day the baby comes out and the mom chases it around until she catches them. Then she has to feed them and take good care of them. ~Lisa, age 4.

~ * ~ * ~ * ~ * ~ * ~ * ~

... I don't know, I'm only three! ~Maddie, age 3.

~ * ~ * ~ * ~ * ~ * ~ * ~

... They come out of a placenta thing called the uterus. They get in there by riding on the sperm all the way to the egg and then the baby starts growing and swimming inside a bag of water. After a while, like 9 months or something, the water bag breaks and the mom gets a C-section and the baby comes out of her stomach. Then the mom and dad get to name the baby and take it home and be happy.
~Dennis, age 12.

~ * ~ * ~ * ~ * ~ * ~ * ~

###

A NOTE FROM THE AUTHOR

I love hearing from my readers, and I answer all my mail personally. If you enjoyed this book would you be kind enough to leave a review on Amazon? Even if it's only a few words - it really does make a difference, and would be very much appreciated.

Simply go to www.Amazon.com and type Kristi Porter into the search bar. Then choose the appropriate story, click reviews, then click create your own review and let me know what you thought.

~ ~ ~

If you would like to receive an automatic email when my next book is released, go to http://eepurl.com/ES3kD to sign up. Your email address will never be shared and you can unsubscribe at any time.

~ ~ ~

Thanks so much for taking the time to read and review my work. It's readers like you that help make my next book even better!

Kristi Porter

ABOUT THE AUTHOR

Kristi Porter has over twenty-five years of experience working with young children, both as a preschool teacher, and as an award winning child care provider. She holds a degree in Early Childhood Education and Development, as well as a national Child Development Associate Credential. In 1999, she was awarded the Governor's Quality Care Award for her outstanding commitment to the care and education of young children.

Always a reader, Kristi never thought much about writing until she entered a writing contest sponsored by the Detroit Free Press. Her story - The Worst Vacation Ever - went on to be published in a travel anthology that was distributed worldwide. This was followed by numerous articles published in local magazines and newspapers. As her love of writing grew, she added adult fiction, how-to books for parents, and short humor pieces to her repertoire.

But kids and writing aren't all Kristi relishes. She also enjoys bicycling, video games, photography, Facebook, and spending time with family. She lives in Michigan.

CONNECT WITH KRISTI ONLINE

Twitter: @KristiPorter3

Facebook: Facebook/Kristi Porter - Author

Website: http://happikamper.weebly.com

Email: Kristiporter03@gmail.com

OTHER BOOKS BY KRISTI PORTER

Available at Amazon.com and bookstores everywhere.

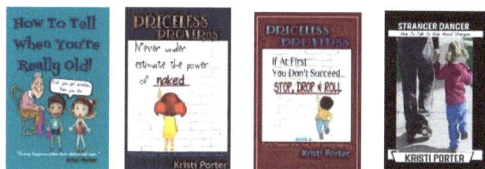

How to Tell When You're Really Old - Funny Happens When Kids Define Old Age, is the result of hundreds of interviews with children ages three to twelve, who were asked to explain how they could tell when someone was really old. Their candid, uncensored, and often hilarious answers will not only make you rethink the aging process, but are sure to become instant favorites for readers of all ages.

~ ~ ~

Priceless Proverbs - Funny Happens When Kids Finish Famous Sayings is a clever collection of words and crayon art created by children of today. Honest and raw, this small book is an utter delight as each old saying or proverb is revised and filtered through the innocent minds of children ages 3 to 12. Sayings that have become so clichéd to we adults, take on a totally new twist as children tend to tell it as it is, and you're certain to find delightful surprises on every page. Highly relatable, this book will make you want to interview the kid closest to you for even more "Priceless Proverbs!"

~ ~ ~

Priceless Proverbs - Book 2, is the second volume of the wildly popular Priceless Proverbs Collection. It features over one hundred additional quotes - wise, entertaining and uncensored - by kids ages three to twelve who were asked to finish well-known proverbs or famous sayings all on their own. Great for anyone that loves children or simply needs a smile to brighten their day.

~ ~ ~

Stranger Danger - How to Talk to Kids About Strangers is a guide to help parents and caregivers of children ages 3-8 teach kids about strangers in a fun, interactive, and age appropriate way - without scaring them. This easy to read, step by step guide gives parents age appropriate words and activities to use with even the youngest of children. Covering everything from who is a stranger, to when and how to fight back, *Stranger Danger - How to Talk to Kids About Strangers* is a must read guide for today's parents.

ACKNOWLEDGEMENTS

I'd like to extend a warm thanks to Lynn Dahl Scholl, Tish Huber Winton, and Sheri Berge, for helping me conduct hundreds of interviews with children over the years. I couldn't have done it without all of you.

Many thanks as well to the White Lake Writers Group for their guidance, encouragement, and support as I sorted through all of those interviews to put this book together.

A special thanks goes out to Tirzah Goodwin, for her awesome cover design; & to my three amazing grandsons for their help with illustrations.

Lots of love, respect and appreciation to my husband for his understanding and support as I spent countless hours in front of the computer, preparing this book for publication.

And to my mom, for always believing in me, encouraging me, and pestering me to finish this and other projects - I love you more than words can say.

And finally, a heartfelt thank you to the children of North Muskegon, who allowed me into their hearts and minds, and gave me a remarkable glimpse into this wonderful world we live in - thru their eyes, their minds, and their perceptions. Priceless.

www.ingramcontent.com/pod-product-compliance
Lightning Source LLC
Chambersburg PA
CBHW040345060426
42445CB00029B/10